WHAT RE'

"Memories, observations, and echoes of the one woman's life are woven like threads throughout Particia Asuncion's spell-binding poetry collection, *Cut on the Bias*. The series of primarily confessional works poems, demonstrate the seams of a woman's world, yet the narrative sense of the poems are collective of stories that grasp much of humankind as a whole. *Cut on the Bias* introduces the reader to the world the author saw surround her, but didn't always have the ability to change . . . One can't help but feel empathy while reading many poems in this collection . . . *Cut on the Bias* is a collection of confession, but within a handful of poems you will begin to see the story of many, maybe even your own."
    Angela M. Carter, author of *Memory Chose a Woman's Body*

"In this collection, Patricia Asuncion blends culture survival with political awareness and poignant emotions. Her work addresses the innermost functions of modern day human existence in a manner that is accessible to readers of all ages and all backgrounds. *Cut on the Bias* is a true poetic manifesto that emanates echoes of Ginsberg's *Howl* and catapults Asuncion into the public eye as one of Virginia's foremost movers and shakers in poetry."
    Nicole Yurcaba, author of *Backwards and Back Words*

"Her history, part of a remarkable fabric weave, is also American history. She keenly watches her own memories, taking her past into her present writing. A mistress of trope with her characteristic inner-city syntax and language, you must take in carefully every line of every poem and remember yourself as Patsy gives you every part of herself. And note her choices of form: from traditional to experimental to hip-hop, she does it all."
    Sara Robinson, *Southern Writers' Magazine* columnist, author of *Two Little Girls in a Wading Pool*, *Stones for Words*, and *Sometimes the Little Town*

"In *Cut on the Bias*, Patsy Asuncion exquisitely evokes a wealth of experiences and emotions that leave the reader deeply touched and primed to creatively step out into a kinder world. Gripping, heart-wrenching, inspiring, Patsy's poems convey a rare depth of feeling and meaning, masterfully crafted."
    Jo Christiane Ledakis, Author of *Wild Sea-Salt of Life*

"Ms. Asuncion's *Cut on the Bias* collection addresses today's socio-political topics head-on and without apology from a very personal perspective. This work speaks for many blended American cultures somehow caught in the middle of progress and not knowing how to reconcile the variety we love about this country and its people. The heart is encouraged by an uplifting positive flight to survive and succeed in a world of conflicting shades, ages, and technologies."
    Michelle O'Hearn, poet, singer-songwriter, author of three poetry chapbooks and producer of three global music CDs

"Poet Patricia Asuncion uses raw expression with unique style that places the reader inside her mind while reading her works."
    Ras Takura, Reggae Dub Poet, Organizer of Jamaica's annual Dis Poem Words & Agro Festival

"Part celebration, part protest, part declaration, part elegy, Asuncion's *Cut on the Bias* revels in sharing "bites of mortality, souvenirs/ of life's sloppy imperfection . . . *Cut on the Bias* teases and reveals threads of many hues and textures, but all make up contemporary life."
    Stan Galloway, author of *Just Married*, James River Writers Award, Founder and Host of Bridgewater International Poetry Festival

In this powerful debut collection, Patricia Asuncion poems bravely walk us through a tough Chicago neighborhood, where a half-Filipino girl, abandoned as an infant by her teenage mother, fights to thrive as she creates her life from the scattered threads of her impoverished immigrant family who seldom showed her love. . . . In poem after poem, Asuncion's poetry and fresh imagery take us on an odyssey to find love and acceptance in this world whose dreams seemingly excluded hers. . . . Using passionate imagery and deft rhythms, Asuncion leads us through her struggle to overcome poverty, exclusion, racism, a dearth of love. That she triumphs despite all of this is astonishing. Hers is an American story, the story of immigrants all over the world.
  Pamela Uschuk, author of *Crazy Love* (American Book Award) and *Blood Flower*

> Sharon,
> To my oldest and dearest who shares some of this journey with me!
> Love,
> Patsy

CUT ON THE BIAS

POEMS BY

PATSY ASUNCION

Laughing *Fire*
p r e s s

Copyright © 2015 Patsy Asuncion

All rights reserved. No part of this book may be reproduced in any form by any electronic or mechanical means including information storage and retrieval systems without written permission from the publisher, except by a reviewer, who may quote brief passages in a review.

ISBN 978-0-9964905-2-8

www.laughingfire.com

patasuncion96@gmail.com
www.patasuncion.wix.com/patsy-asuncion
www.facebook.com/patricia.asuncion.58
YouTube Channel: go to Patricia Asuncion or UCiI15rI-R04et_XYu70A_Hug

Table of Contents

Hand-Me-Down Threads

Personal Raw Edge – Unfinished, Cut Edge

Jungle Gym 1
Back Talk 2
Everything and Nothing 3
Peace Makers 5
Street Signs 6
First Kiss 8
Scrapbook 9
Reflection 11
small price 12
Lost At Sea 14
Jalopy 16
Head Lines 18
Bearing Fruit 19
Tramp 21
Believe 22

Family Ombre – Closely Related Color Tones, Light to Dark

Caste Out 27
Her Anthem for a Soldier Come Home 29
Fallen Leaves 30
wallet 32
Late Night Show 34
Locked 35
"When you're dead, you're dead," 37
Enigma 38
A Cut Above 40

empty fridge   41
emptying   43
Living Will   44
Strum Drum   45
Grandma's In Da House   46
A Sort of Self   49

Turned Inside Out

Social Slash/Spread – Cutting and Spreading Open Along Cutline for Fullness

Twitnomenon   53
Twitter Self-Portrait   55
Rock, Paper, iPad   56
Friendling   58
PR   60
Power Begins in the Cloud   61
Crossroad   63
What's-her-name   64
Dead Head   65
Time After Time   67
False Face   68
Strip Mall Apocalypse   69
Food Fights   70
Ew!   72
Class Act   74

Political Whiskers – Tiny, Frayed Threads From Raw Seam Edges

Double Take   77
Comfort of Elsewhere   78
Keffiyeh   81

World Hunger   82
Blood Money   84
High-Rent Neighborhood   86
No Sense Nonsense   87
Pigmentocracy   88
Flip Side   89
Tempest   92
March 11, 2011   93
Old Miss Libertas   94
Writing on the Wall   95
Corrupted Innocence   96
Math for Girls Counts   97

Global Darning – Repairing Holes or Worn Areas

Lunch Encounter   101
Mixed Woodland   102
Universal Language   103
Cold War Corner   105
Living Large   106
Unseen Seen   107
Newlyweds 96 & 95   108
Global Spectrum   109
Penny the Shrimp   110
United We Stand   111
No Dead Roots   112
Openhanded   113
Way of Looking   114
No Pain, All Gain?   116
One Line to Live   117

Personal Raw Edge – Unfinished, Cut Edge

*We're always attracted to the edges of what we are,
out by the edges where it's a little raw and nervy.*

E.L. Doctorow

Jungle Gym

The inner-city beachfront unleashed
gushing fire hydrants mobbed
by neighborhood kids in underwear
for swimsuits, flooded streets

their ocean. They were hard at play
in pavement playgrounds – gangways
for ball games, abandoned cars in weed
lots their forts, and rooftops their hide-

go-seek park. Music was cornered
under street lights by doo-wop dudes
with pompadours who dazzled chicks
with beehives. They be-bopped

together to transistor radio tunes. Slum
kids know no-frill fun. They makeshift,
quick-and-dirty improvise, and dump-
dive prosperity where they find it.

Back Talk

When I was a kid, I could scoot around
on my mental roller skates to any city block
in Chicago and speak the language of the
hood, the words which colored that culture.

I spoke enough Polish to order the best
pierogis or tell off a punk Polack. I used my
basic Spanish to shop at the local Puerto Rican
mercado and Italian to flirt with cute Dego boys.

Foreign phrases common to these old neighborhoods
stuck with me – *vanffancul*, (with rude arm gestures),
jak się masz, dónde está el baño, dziękuję, ¿Qué pasa?
They flew effortlessly off my tongue.

The years have now confused my links to language
with detours to other definitions and passing phrases,
with traffic delays around newly-constructed words.
Old lingo now lingers on street corners I can't find.

Everything and Nothing

It was the best of times, it was the worst of times, it was the age of wisdom, it was the age of foolishness... it was the season of Light, it was the season of Darkness.

A Tale of Two Cities, Charles Dickens

High school graduation
our singular event in 1964, our season
to make a difference.

Believing
new heavyweight champ Ali – we could
float like a butterfly, sting like a bee, we could
rise from poverty like the Beatles, we could
enjoy equal opportunity in the Promise Land of new laws.

That was the banner year.
Johnson's Civil Rights Act
thickened conviction –
    power to the people was possible.
Poitier's Oscar
Martin Luther King's Nobel Peace Prize
Frazier's Gold
– all in '64,
in-your-face confrontation with convention.
Fresh-faced, virtuous Medicare
helped the sick and elderly.
Even big tobacco took a hit
from the Surgeon General.
    I have a dream pulsed our senses.

Yet, it was the first year of Viet Nam,
a twenty-year war
coupled with twenty years of domestic violence –
King's assassination
Riots

Kent State and Jonestown – knuckling
us into bruised disbelief of the Establishment.

The '90s saw the demise of Russia and the Cold War,
but homegrown rampage
raged on – Columbine, Oklahoma City, Waco.

These past fifty years, our parents' work ethic
anchored us.
We made a difference
through our labor, which defined our identity.
Retirement is merely redirection.

That same 1964 *I can*
attitude carries over to this new century
of live stream, Blu-ray, nooks, smartphones, face transplants,
in-vitro kidneys, stem cell livers, even asteroid Pluto. We are
the high-def seniors of the world, engaged
and running like the Eveready Bunny.

Peace Makers

As best high school buds and bright center of the universe,
Millie and I fought walk-talk duels, all over '60s Chicago –
North-side ganglands to Old Town yippee-hippie shops.

Like omniscient teens, confident in our blueprint of
global peace, we gestured to pigs, dirty cops with kick-me
targets on their backs put there by peaceful hippies.

We shouted at TV's Tricky Dicky Nixon, the catalyst
for public corruption, and cheered draft dodgers as saintly
martyrs of truth. Black-and-white rules rocked our world.

We survived the '68 riots in our short-tempered
neighborhood. At carbon-copy class reunions, we traded
vacant conversations, which were polished summaries,

replete with photo highlights and footnotes of creaky
physical changes. After the rehearsed revelations, we'd
recoil to merry-go-round lives with the same stale

headlines. Time has not changed news, or the probability
of new. Activists to time watchers, we baby boomers now
wait for the next generation to bring us closer to peace.

Street Signs

From my gangway, my life story
strolls past neighbors on stoops
to cool from the Windy City's
steam-bath summer, yelling over

transistors at kids to watch for cars
as they play in the street. The name
of the Jewish butcher is buried in
my years of city soot, but I see his

plucked chickens dripping in the
window, their blood a tasty soup in
Great Depression bread lines. Down
the block, there's Casey, the Polish

grocer, ready to cut me a pound
of round for my stepmother's routine
hangover, like a steak for a fighter's
bruised eye. The coin laundry at the

busy corner waits for me to drag the
bag to wash family rags as I hang
with bums who sleep there full cycle.

We nod but never eye each other, the
shame too thick. New money solicits
worry-free success stories in the windows
of these embattled Chicago bricks. Faint

lines of the butcher store haunt the fringes
of new fancy lofts. Newly frosted and ivy-
covered, Casey's windows conceal a
well-heeled home. The laundromat is

long gone, so too the movie house where I
won free accordion lessons and the five and ten
where I dreamed of working one day. While
today's dreams are bigger than my dime

store ambitions, my loyalty to da Cubbies hails
from north side radio days. Fresh from the butcher
or local grocer still beat today's big-box shops.
These resilient buildings remain my framework.

First Kiss

Our two-week camp on the lake
was a temporary pass from poverty,
paid by the city. Still half tomboy,

I came to conquer woods, fight
more than wild life on the street.

On the way to shore, I set eyes
on my first love, a budding fugitive
there to beat jail time for gang wars.

Tall, brooding Brando magnetism,
he evoked a cat-mouse edginess.

Instantly, my bad-ass damsel became
the pink princess and his punk criminal,
the frog prince. Without trumpeting

my intentions, I worked to win every
camp game in hopes of his notice.

Time evaporated into a farewell
dance. The pauper prince asked me
for a slow one, close and tight. My head

tried to avoid stepping on him, but my
heart took control when we kissed.

The bus ride home lasted four fairytale
years. His enlistment cheated yet another
judge. School was my ticket from the hood.

Scrapbook

Fifty years folded into
the present, I relive my first
serious injury – the sharp slice

across my ankle, metal
on bone, as I pump pedals
madly in my cousin's toy car

like Mario Andretti for the win.
I don't see the gushing crimson
until my escape. Kneecaps

pop corned in layers of fossilized
scars, the gravel digs ditches
into both knees as I slide to win

Chicago's slow-pitch ballgames
pretending to be celebrated Cubby,
Sammy Sosa.

I inherited Dad's varicose veins,
but mine are less angry crooks
behind both kneecaps.

The scooped purple moon
behind my left knee,
is a vestige of my worst

collision, a slam-stop by
railroad ties like a crash dummy
mangled at breakneck speed.

I also have a collection of
deliberate scars from cutting
bony outcrops, like pulling weeds.

There's a slight smile on my
left knee while under
the knife, the doctor failing

to mention I was his first
laser patient. Other spots pepper
my shins and thighs, too many

to name, but all irreversible
bites of mortality, souvenirs
of life's sloppy imperfection.

Reflection

Water splashes and I am a kid again,
awash in the crowd of summer

children running in the city park
fountain, like seal pups on rocks

frolicking in the ocean spray. We
tumble in laughter of immigrant

languages. Raw fun needs no
translation. But, the fountains

and hydrants were silenced abruptly
like a snuffed-out candle, after

polio was proclaimed a ruthless
epidemic by the 1952 Chicago Tribune,

ten years before school vaccines.
Decades later, friends who survived are

still tortured by viral re-awakenings,
like one long PTSD nightmare. As

I again see the showers wash over tiny
faces in the fount, I am grateful
for the return of young innocence.

small price

To survive is to find some meaning in the suffering.
                                    Friedrich Nietzsche

Filipino brothers dangled on Yankee acceptance –
the sweet carrot of hard work allowed them

to forget their children like starfruit rotting
at the bottom of the fridge. We three mestizo cousins,

forced into siblings by survival – one toddler scrambled
eggs from a stepstool, another became the three-year-old

nanny to the baby, and we all learned hangover
mixes for White, AWOL mothers.

In school, ball fields and gangs, we pocketed family
secrets like magicians, but our battle fatigue

ricocheted nasty side effects –
AIDS   variety-pack substance abuse   serial marriages.

We never found parents, a safe place from
hostile fall-out in our heads, and buried our grief-

stained memories with the disease-riddled
youngest, a necessary excuse for survival.

The child chef has lost his mother, his father
and now his baby brother. My losses of parents make

me the matriarch of the mestizo side. We two survivors
don't speak much with little in common

above the water line, just midnight replays of the mental internment camp from our childhood.

Lost At Sea

For whatever we lose (like a you or a me),
It's always our self we find in the sea.
                                               e.e. cummings

    I am struck by the only snapshot   I have
of my teenage   biological mother.
Shoulders folded over the tidal weight
of premature responsibility, she hunches

    at the edge of the frame   apart
from me on my daddy's lap
    on the other side of the photo's world
where family loses touch.

She and I stare, stark as twin coffins
while my father   poses   for the camera
with an immigrant's big-toothed pride.
I harbor an early voice,
vague, a foghorn from memory's riptides
        Let her cry

as I lie alone in darkness. I don't
know my age, but I can still feel this backwash
of vacant loss going back,
    before my birth.

These two clues are   all
I have of the   back-alley teenager
who pushed me into this world   the hook
that entices then lets me go.

My hospital records show they
were married   all properly homogenized
for public viewing   before I
was born   but divorce records confuse
any clear story, except

    the word *abandonment*, less than two
years after my birth. The ink on the docs, dried
decades ago, a permanent tattoo
on my skin, hidden in shame.

Beyond this physical evidence, I have   nothing
of my early months with her, nothing –
    no pictures of the two of us,   none.
Holding me, did she smile or make funny faces?
    No baby mementos,   none.

Did she buy me a doll or toy guitar like hers?
    No hand-me-downs,   none.
Did she have a favorite hat or special ring?
This nothingness only seems to deepen
        my longing, large as the lunar sea.

Jalopy

She was stolen   shiny new   outside
a tenement for a joy ride   then abandoned
in a back alley   No anti-theft devices
in those days   just next of kin   to fender
troublemakers   When they found her
they thought she was lucky   just
a busted headlight   bloody dents
and pigeon-toed tires   probably
the reason thieves   dumped her

Once healed   she proved   a good car
who kept good traction   whenever
she drove her stepmother   home
from the neighborhood   tap   Mechanics
saw her potential   caught her interest
with books   Interior lights   a tough
engine   ensured   high performance
in school despite   being   left
alone a lot   on the street

Tomboy antics in the alleys   scarred
all four tires but she put up   a poker-face
Two crashes   shorting her electrical
started migraines   every time she used
her turn signals   Surgery on ball joints
and quality oil seemed to quiet   cranky
squeaks   when she rolled   She paid
attention   keeping her trim   in top shape
to slow depreciation   unlike some friends

Maintenance doesn't stop   life's odometer
    Rust spots   on her once flawless finish
increased   each winter   Young cracks

in her underbody   began puckering her
mainframe   Cheap gas had been   no
problem but then started   upsetting her gut
Chronic allergies insisted   more air filter
changes   Not surprised   each time she
was traded   She   didn't choose   her owners

Sold now as   vintage   she is   adept
a classic from the day   the only one
to make it   out of the old neighborhood
While memory settings   have lost old
details   she recalls   important choices
    running even in bad weather   starting
    while missing parts   finding her way
    regardless of   confusing road signs
    optimizing   her standard   components

Head Lines
(Self-Portrait)

Fleshed copies of my Filipino immigrant
father's, my gnarly, arthritic hands are
tough, not afraid of hard work. He bleached

his to blend while I, a prize fighter from
a Chicago ghetto, lifted my fists against
the Great White Way. Sometimes my pride

throbs like an ingrown nail insisting on one
direction even when it causes pain. But, my
ego crest holds on despite odds, keeping

me as organized and focused as a surgical laser.
I germinate in the soil of my senses, fed by
curiosity, prismatic, created in layered facets,

my need to shape the new or fix what's broken.
Like Hydra, I am a contortion of contradictions,
imagining rejuvenation from sickness and

poverty. But, seconds later, I become the brooding
serpent spreading poisonous bile in a worried
swamp. I order my stiff hands into an obedient

salute as a young recruit's to keep my earned
place in line, unlike my father who did nothing
to keep others from cutting in front of him.

Bearing Fruit

Let the past go. A simply abundant world awaits.
                                        Sarah Ban Breathnach

Hero Jose Rizal Mercado, is the Philippino
George Washington. Each Rizal Day,
I became fiery Chita Rivera in Broadway's

West Side Story, my fancy patent leather shoes
flashing the cha-cha and mambo with my
dad in Chicago hotel ballrooms. I cherish those

childhood big band celebrations, the only times
we touched. A daughter never hugged, I believed
the emotional world was A-flat-lined

scientific proof, documented by my trials.
It wasn't until my adult studies showed
the world was, in fact, abundantly round, that

I initiated the hugging. Dad hugged back like a
gangly teenager, awkward in adult sizes. Evolution
prepares the strongest, honing their internal GPS

to success. The Latin Kings and Gaylords, marked
gang turfs, survival zones for members only. Everyone
knew what streets to avoid, except me. Having blood

cousins as gang lieutenants, I walked wherever
I damn well pleased. Gangbangers saw me as
just a nerdy girl, a compliant lab rabbit in its cage.

I didn't drive until thirty. Traffic was just a still life
painting, especially rush hour. My cousins hated

I'd walk to the other side of Chi-town to hang out
with the rival Waps, but I loved Italian olive oil
flowing from every pore. Jukebox Sinatra and cold
beers were my sixteen-year-old freedom march flags.

Now, my perspective is caught on the silver-wire
fence around my heart. Abundance brings me mangos
and hummus, better than beer, and poets, better than street

punks. My surviving cousin and I signed a treaty,
resigned to a dead reckoning of different choices in fleshy
rummage and soulful speculations, much like

the native Hawaiians' practice of *Ho'oponopono*
and similar to my dad's pre-colonial world,
before the mark of the Catholic cross.

Tramp

We met in the 1925 house with creaky old-timer floors,
    at the top of the only Florida hill.
There was a big crabgrass yard filled with
    orange and pecan trees, too many to pick.
Never worried, you made a game of the rotting fruit,
    burying it as fallen treasure.

Remember our one-month-11-state trip to Mexico
    in the unforgiving heat of high summer?
What a time we had all squeezing in front of
    the rented A/C box at the Vegas campsite!
I still see the kind wrinkle of a woman at the Tijuana border
    who gave you water on the street.

The great outdoors transported you to your personal heaven,
    a guy contented by earthy scents and scenes.
No wonder you hated to bathe,
    to lose the crusty mementos of walks in the woods.
For such a man's man, you were quivery jello
    whenever you heard the meekest crackle in the sky!

But, you were an ornery ball of fire
    who quieted me with unconditional love.
When I was playfully happy or still-life sad,
    you were my steadfast companion in any weather.
The wide grins of our uncommon friendship
    always made my face hurt.

I've not looked at another little red-haired mutt
    without seeing you these past twenty years.
You are with me on every walk in the woods,
    just ahead as my vigilant scout.
You are here at day's end,
    still the soft cushion for my tired bones.

Believe

Sheets   as doors
between rooms in our tenement
Terminal linoleum
riddled with primordial dirt   creeping cracks

Erie outreach program   gave chances
to other worlds Once
I stayed with a family with
clean feet and toenails   saw my first

lawn   I remember   wanting   a home-home
with green grass   spotless floors
Believing   in more
merely magical thinking

I never admitted caring we had no
Christmas tree   At eight   I figured Santa
was a fake   No sugarplum fairies for me
just socks and underwear

Not to spoil it for younger kids   I went along
for the ride   Santa at another Erie event
Twinkling trees   yes trees   lined the long hall
tables piled high   in sweets

In the center of the back wall   alleged Santa
seated upon a bejeweled throne
Closer inspection   (I mean casual glance)
revealed   a real snow-white beard   shiny

(not department store plastic)   leather boots
I could tell   Genuine fur trimmed his suit
real ribboned packages overflowed
The youngest on his knee   I checked every

move for flawless proof
When my name was called
I exaggerated   my measured walk   toward Santa
so no one thought   I was a baby   On his lap

tiny rainbow trickles sprinkled me   his eyes
a safe place to rest   Then he asked what I'd waited
for all night Patsy what do you want for Christmas
I knew   this rent-by-the-night Santa

couldn't give me   what I wanted   but in case   I
answered   *A cheerleader's baton*
I hadn't told anybody   anywhere   not my parents
not teachers   not Erie volunteers   no one

The unimaginable   happened   He pulled out
a brand new baton   just for me   I hugged this
man   no Santa   as hard as I could   as long as I
dared   How could he have known   my secret

unless he was genuine   It was then   I knew
Santa is real
I've lost the baton   but his genuine gift remains
Belief transforms

Santa is real
my home with green grass
and clean floors is
real too

Family Ombre – Closely Related Color Tones, Light to Dark

Parents are like shuttles on a loom. They join the threads of the past with threads of the future and leave their own...patterns as they go.

Fred Rogers

Caste Out

My urban ghetto was a soup kitchen of immigrants –
Black, White, Hispanic, Slavic stirring up their own
gang turfs, crews and church creeds. Threatened,

like feeling a switch blade to throat, nobody crossed
territory marked in piss by different dogs.
Dark mahogany, my Filipino father honed an appetite

for white women – ate at least three wives I heard,
two blondes and an Irish red-head, my teen mother
who fled before my first birthday. His American

dream came at a stabbing price, serial divorces.
As a child, piercing stares, deliberate as daggers,
were thrown my way, disguised as routine

pastime, merely glances from zoo visitors
inspecting a curious cub. But, their surveillance
skittered when I looked their way, like a wolf

spider discovering it's the one now being hunted.
Eyes zigzagged scars across father to stepmother,
then pretended to settle on others. They scanned

me last for telltale moves and my milk-chocolate
features to spit out right after we left.
Civilized bias, polite as afternoon tea, discouraged me.

There were break-ups by college boys after meeting
their parents who'd skewer me with steel words like
Don't get involved with her, son, face the color facts.

To this day, questions from strangers about
my heritage in *Where you from?* really intending
What are you? After auditions, I'd get *Sorry, you're*

not the right look for us. Even my in-laws
warned *Son, we're worried about more
problems if you have children.*

Bigotry cut through white-washed walls
to the full-blooded Filipino world that erased me –
shunned at celebrations, cut from Tagalog dialogue,

forgotten in family headlines and denied my birthrights.
There was no need for my parents to hint, joke or
talk about invasive scrutiny because each had

identification cards – one for Brown and one for
White exclusive memberships. I held a Green card –
alien residence, subject to restrictions without notice.

Her Anthem for a Soldier Come Home

You enlisted at 39, a fat Filipino immigrant,
for a chance to fight invaders back home
like a brown-skinned John Wayne. Your
new land strapped you in a girdle to trim

your girth and made you a flame thrower,
fueled by your own anger against the Japs.
In a segregated unit, you returned home –
the first and last time, to set fire to caves

where you had played, to roast the enemy,
then hidden deep in once virgin jungles,
like an infestation of vermin. The dead
and tortured half-dead of faces familiar

made it easier to kill and to suffer your
own sacrifices in silence – mind sores,
jungle rot and government double-dealing.
Paraded at recruitment, banners of benefits

and naturalization were muddied in post-
war streets of Asian prejudice. Color
denied a hard-fought place in line for
veterans, but you beat the odds, like

a big-time lottery winner. You became
a citizen with some medals to shout your
worth. You imbibed the new world sacraments –
language, liquor and alabaster ladies.

That trademark tried-and-true smile
with a VFW cap plastered on top, still
speaks (in English only) of allegiance to an
adopted country that can do no wrong.

Falling Leaves

*Let us spend one day as deliberately as Nature,
and not be thrown off the track by every nutshell
and mosquito's wing that falls on the rails.*
Henry David Thoreau

Leaves fall
making patterns
of burnt colors
on the cold ground
of my life.
Endless days of
raking them into piles
against the winds
bury my smiles
for I focus on
the tidiness
rather than
the laughter in life's messiness.
But, life is found
in broken wings,
in cracked nutshells,
even in piles of dead leaves.
Life refuses to be tidied
by the stubborn rules
of my old handmade rake.
The leaf of my father
hung stubbornly,
refusing to join his brothers
on the ground
and as I waited
for the silent hush
of his fall,
I forced myself

to stop raking
long enough
to see the beauty
in his changing colors,
to laugh with him
as he spun
in the wind
from his frail stem.

wallet

The old man clutches his worn-out billfold stuffed
with young dreams of a kinder world as if he's been
holding on to the winning ticket to Fat City.

There's his stained, original 1936 social security
card, which trumpets Roosevelt's promise of tranquil
retirement, a final resting place on this side of the

ground, without hint of today's Medicaid madness
and malaise. The billfold also holds his young smile
captured by automated renewal on his license

laminated into the next millennium, like a
cryopreserved head. Mechanical mail didn't think to
ask questions of a ninety-something who dreams

of buying a Cadillac. His proudest possession is the
gold-plated, lifetime VFW card that hails service to his
adopted country, like a twenty-one gun salute each

morning. It permits him to boast of his bravery
and importance against invaders of his homeland. But,
gold-plated isn't enough to defeat his lingering wounds

and nightmares. The voter's registration card chronicles
a perfect-voting record of a life-long staunch Republican
who believes only in black and white, like starched

patriotic principles without one wavering wrinkle. Set
rules were ever accepted, never questioned. Mixed
among his contents are dead scraps of discolored paper

with scribbled phone numbers of long-forgotten faces
who don't visit him in his nursing-home solitude, except
through the treasures of this faithful leather memoir.

Late Night Show

Dazed dribble streams
my mind like a late night
talk show drones stale jokes.

Gray TV-land insomnia
holds my sleeplessness
captive, a war criminal

whose eyes are pried
open by midnight madness.
Like water torture, tears

force my sinuses to scream,
my head to explode with fear.
Daybreak's change of guard

brings different torments,
but my body endures while
my one true pain is held

in solitary confinement.
My father is dying. Some
part of me is dying too.

Locked

I

The Club on the steering wheel threatened
thieves, so too the boot on the tires, like cops'
flashing lights warning to detour or die, but hunger
to own something, anything, even a clunker,
rendered the man's car security useless to street
punks pumped for joy rides, big-chested manhood.

II

He installed four bolts on the front and back
of his house to baffle would-be burglars and to keep
family secrets from public peephole. Nobody knew
about the binges and battles nor the bruises
concealed next day when the bolts unlocked
like escaped convicts dodging floodlights.

III

Thick chain around the man's neck
meant more than peacock flirtation, rather
a chain link fence around his hard-boiled resolve
to survive on foreign turf regardless of the toll. He'd
fought bosses, distanced from his children, left
wives. Nobody got close to his self-made cell.

IV

Forty years locked in a fight, the padlocked
door to the man's separate bedroom prevented
his spouse from harming him. Ordinary, household
items had become macabre missiles – blistering pans,
splintering glass, poisoning cleaners. The domestic
war was deadlier than the foreign war he'd fought.

V

At last secure in a sealed bronze urn, boxed
on a daughter's back shelf, he's forgotten unless
shuffled like dusty nuisance while the living rummage
for misplaced possessions. Poverty, prejudice,
pain dead bolted his life. In death, he can take his
first breath of freedom.

"When you're dead, you're dead,"

you said when examining final plans. Ash seemed more
sense than a box. You saw no need to gather for goodbyes.

A decade has dissolved without notice, but yesterday your
gnarled fingers cooked gingered cabbage and ramen, your fragrance

familiar to my melancholy kitchen. On trash day, you push
the mower, replete with cans jiggling, to the curb – too far

for your frail legs, not your well-preserved dignity. I suspect
you dress in colorful fanfare to cultivate looks, strutting

like a world wrestling champ in shock-wave patterns. You greet
every woman with a sexy, exuberant smile like a Chippendale,

dollars falling from your G-string. Your chronic complaints of
your brother boil over, but you never skip cutting his hair,

conversing in Ilocano as you did as boys in Luzon. I took your
car keys after a near-miss, only to find your spare for adventures

behind my back with your ninety-somethin' kid brother, two
rebellious teens full of themselves. Dad, I don't believe what you

said about life ending in bones. I'm living proof. You resonate in
my spunky backbone, a water buffalo slugging through rice paddies;

you stoke my belly's fire to be the prize in every cracker jack box;
you techno-color my garish glee in the outrageous outfits I parade.

Enigma

My father came
in the footsteps
of a post-war survivor
distracted by demons.

He seemed to care
in obscure ways,
difficult to discern
as I much preferred

tangible hugs.
He did his dutiful best
to provide for me by hard
work, his insignia for love.

Since he decoded caring as
Maintenance, he checked
the frequency of my bowel
movements as a baby

to measure my well-being
like a mechanic
dips an oil stick. He once
showed emotion when he

punched trash cans
in the alley after I had
an all-nighter prom, an
unfamiliar tradition

in the islands. Still shocked
by his departure from military
restraint, I don't know if he
was angry or relieved

when I came home so late.
As an adult, I settled for
the unsolved mystery that
was my father. Beginning

with hugs, I cared for
the old man until his
last days in the ways
I had wanted for myself.

A Cut Above

Aunt Isa's tenement flat
doubled as hair salon to the stars
every strand a work of art
  just like the magazines

worth it to the dreamers
  climbing all those stairs
    never spying sleeping bums
      never smelling pissy booze

dark roots to blonde goddess
faded to bee-hive bombshell
bottle and brush   her sacraments
clientele   her born-again believers

her potions floated full-color
  high above the weight
of hand-me-downs
  and slum quarters

I watched her make-overs
    develop from single strands of belief
I learned her self-taught craft
    to design my own haut monde.

empty fridge

our old Harvest Gold GE housed
invisible villains   lurking in the litter

gummy peanut butter
   disguised   as faceless mold between shelves
open white bread
   transformed   into furry pet rocks
half-eaten slice of pizza
   abandoned in an extra-large delivery box
a single slimy black banana
   left for dead under putrid fruit
half-consumed mega-sized colas
   lying helter skelter   like wasted partiers
gray bologna
   hardened twisted   like a career criminal

my empty-nester Whirlpool features
politically-correct labeled cuisine

condiments pure as unsullied soldiers
   in recyclable bottles   at attention in the doors
happy-heart meats and cheeses
   triathletes of salt sugar fat
breads buns with no make-up tricks
   doing roll-ups on the middle rack
local all-American produce
   squeaky clean   aligned in drawers
bikini-dream-driven drinks water
   without weight or unreadable chemicals
organic spreads touting
   virgin purity like a presidential hopeful

I prefer our old fridge grumbling like
   a rude teenager
brimming with the leavings of life
oh, I much prefer it to mine now
filled with its lineup of tidy emptiness

emptying

hole in the bucket
nothing to mend it
cells die and unknit
brain gaps deepen slits

who's that he asks
what's that he rasps
same queries alas
response wears mask

memory pours out
new files don't route
recall in doubt
facts blurred throughout

who's that I pry
sad stares reply
blank eyes don't lie
mere shell I spy

decline just creeps
drip, drop, he seeps
lost love I weep
raw tears, knee-deep

Living Will

The prepackaged end plan
is absent in progressive disease.
There are no casserole gifts, no flowers,
no family rituals as funeral markers.
The unexpected is expected each day.

Shards of pain remain in shattered
safety glass like tears trapped in an ice storm.
Routines unravel in the slow drip of dying,
dicey as an erosion before a landslide.

After the shockwave, I caught fresh
breath before I relocated my internal compass.
I've had to redraw my maps, but mile
markers indicate a new route to life
while on the way to dying.

Strum Drum

I

Guitar picks scatter   like breadcrumbs to a past.
Vintage guitars hang on walls.   Dusty with neglect,
    an electric sulks in the corner,   the hurt too raw.

Tremor had intruded.   Terrorizing militant muscles,
    frozen limbs were   blocked from plucking.
War imprisoned the music   inside   him.

He'd sat for hours   exploring each guitar's voice.
Strumming strings like old friends   he played to their subtle strengths.
    Now the room echoed   cluttered emptiness.

II

Buried deep brain   wires subdued   defiant shakes.
Resurrected, instruments and muse   restored order
    to passion misplaced.

Strings resonate   grateful for old friendships.
Familiar notes   clear out cobwebs   restore space.
The studio echoes   wall-to-wall   musical banderoles.

His lifeblood is   recaptured   in staccato moments.
He's learning to play   in contemporary tempo   right
on the downbeat.

Grandma's In Da House
True Story

I was looking to read
Find folks of like mind
Share poetry of life
Give and take in kind

I came to the house
Thinkin' it was word
I was first one there
Felt a twinge absurd

The door man asked
Do you need the stage
I didn't know why
He looked so amazed

I felt out of place
When I saw who showed
Pierced parts and inks
Was their tribal code (last two lines, 3X)

Such loud-ass music
Right up in my ear
And I don't know why
The BOX boomed so near

Words acted out loud
No tunes ever bleed
Folks come to the house
To hear poets read (3X)

The room's very young
So why's grandma here?
A culture brand new
I felt a bit fear

But, each said hello
In a friendly way
I wanted to stick
Hear what they'd say (3X)

When the first got up
I knew why the beat
The rhythm and word
had turned up the heat (3X)

I never heard rap
Or hip hop new
Prejudice lives in
us old ladies too (3X)

So I took an ear
To the words he said
While others joined in
The chorus he led

They were movin'
To the beat…beat
Words were smokin'
To the heat…heat

The speak was flyin'
And all understood
There's one group brain
Power to the hood (3X)

My turn came up
I tried to back out
Said I don't do you
So what up, they shout

My poetry spoke
Quiet filled the room
Poets one and all
Nevermore assume (last two lines, 3X)

I was one of them
They were part of me
We were all poets
In the same posse (last two lines, 3X)

I was asked to come back
In a couple of weeks
And learn more ways to
To hear poets speak (4X)

A Sort of Self
Soliloquy

It's quiet here   wherever I am
a kind of quiet I've never met
with breathing room   between thoughts

to sort myself   to look back on myself
a different angle   in the mirror of myself.

I wish I'd been safely parented   before I
parented. Bad habits never died they just
got passed on   to the next gen.

I mourn not having a   maternal moon
to guide my efforts with my children.

Long after they found   their own ways
I did learn to forgive myself   when I
accepted that I was a   mosaic mother.

Perfectionist   critic   five-star general
mixed with   nurturer   protector   muse.

It took me more than fifty years to
find my own true love   a giving guy
who accepted   every part of me.

I think now it took me decades   to have
myself   so I could have him.

I know the best of my life was the
last of my life   when I filtered crystal
clear importance   from dark chatter of the day.

My centerpiece of living large was unlocking
the door to   creativity   at every stage of age.

Picasso said *it takes one   a long time
to become young,* to see with fresh eyes
to play on new paths   to breathe life into dreams.

My only regret is that I didn't learn sooner
to choose beginnings   not accept endings.

Social Slash/Spread – Cutting and Spreading Open Along Cutline for Fullness

Two quite opposite qualities equally bias our minds – habits and novelty.

Chuck Palahniuk

Twitnomenon

Increasingly outnumbered by *Tweeple*,
conversationalists are becoming extinct
like dinosaurs on the social media moon.
One *friendapalooza* can recruit
hundreds in a nanosecond to the *Twitosphere*.
Just one of these *twewbies* can grab
more by hosting a *friendscrapping*, like
swapping keys with virtual friends.
The *Hivemind* grows exponentially, forcing
out the old queen bee's order.

Twitterflies have many followers,
often becoming part of the *twiterrati*.
Despite *twettiquette*, there are reckless
bulltwits, *drunktwitters*, and *trashtweeters*.
Twaffic is jammed like a bad L.A. day
with *tweetsults*, *mistweets*, *twitterage*.
Twishing and *twittworking* can be
dangerous, especially to naïve *neweeters*.

Searching for *twitterphoria* and higher *twitrank*,
tweeterboxes in overdrive, risk becoming *tweetaholics*
by thumbing wildly in *drive-thru-tweets*,
drive-by-tweets, *retweets*, and *detweets*.
Often *twitterpated* with tell-tale hand rash, some opt
for *twabstinence* or *InnerTwitter* to recover from
lost weekends. Those in denial hunger for more
twitterapps, seeking *BiggerTwitter* and *FollowersForSale*.
In the name of *twart*, *twitterature* has flowered
into 140-character *twaikus*, *poetweets*, and novels
in serial *tweets*.

The *tweet* goes on, the *tweet* goes on.
Tweets keep going faster every day –
La de da de de, la de da de da.
Tweets keep pounding a rhythm to the brain –
La de da de de, la de da de da.
The *tweet* goes on, the *tweet* goes on.

Note: all italicized do exist.

Twitter Self-Portrait
(140 characters)

smiles long coming

across childhood scars

past full-grown mistakes

between too many wars

I now find joy

in dirty water

no magic

just well-read eyes

Rock, Paper, iPad

The E-landscape transforms the old into mountains
of text messages, riverbeds of search engines, skies

lit by cell phone glow, all by surgical strike   nothing
of the past   no phone booths, no libraries, no paper

for reference as a walking stick on new ground.
Digital natives touch screens – zoom in, point, click,

shuffle like   a sleeping chromosome suddenly awakened
by a computer click. Even before language bubbles form

above the heads of toddlers, they reach for laptops   fingers
flipping pixelated pages and scrolling   frontiers in a flash.

Hard-copy traditionalists   preferring John Wayne
black and whites, claim knowledge   sticks on paper sheets

like a handheld compass pointing to actual, uneven ground.
Pages let you   feel   the depth of the river   see

the journey in mile markers   focus on the climb to the top
of the rocky   inkscape. Tech screens have their   virtual place

in the new world order. Computers are pinch-hitters for users
sorting   mountains of files, supplying gear for   special needs

and outfitting small-pond to big-game interests, entertainment
to enterprise. Instagram gratification, and exotic places

from home   attract   E-enthusiasts. The old hand game,
Rock, Paper, Scissors has climatized into Rock, Paper, iPad.

Rock beats iPad for tradition.
Paper beats iPad for simplicity.
iPad beats paper for speed.

Friendling

Social media has redefined
self-worth in measures not
measured by internal notches,
like a metronome for honest

heartbeats, but by accounting
records of *follows*, *friends*
and *likes*. Like a peeping
Tech-Tom, *follows* allow

watchng someone without
being friends. Fairytale
profiles can be *shared* in
the virtual world of voyeurs,

with no flirty foreshadow or
live commentary. So friends
can like and others can follow,
faster than speed-dating,

without ever sharing air –
a form of anonymous intimacy,
an efficient method of world
involvement without time-

consuming, actual interaction.
Audience selector and *block*
features promote world peace
by eliminating face-to-face

confrontation or messy real-time
improvisation. Controversial
explanation is assassinated by
the stealth computer. The profile

picture's executive producer
has final say over timeline,
events, and groups so interior
life stays an Internet away.

Discomforts and disparities
are censored with a click
of the spam key. Reality becomes
a manageable board game.

PR

The personals pitch lonely hearts
like used cars in the classifieds,
by touch-up salesmanship.

Social drinker slurs
into daily happy hours
and lost wino weekends.

Young, fifty and fit
sags to tire middles
and stretchmark retreads.

Brown hair and blue eyes
cover receding grays
and soda-bottle squints.

Love of fine arts turns
to random reruns
at the dollar theatre.

Like a gambler hooked on
a one-arm bandit machine,
the lonesome look for one big love,

the one ad for the dream-come-true
used car with little mileage and maintenance
that starts when you turn the key.

Power Begins in the Cloud

When the Cloud became
tangible in 2008 it flung out its arms,
a sci-fi messiah bringing the fringes
into the fold. A heaven-on-earth Big Easy –
self-driving cars, automated data
sharing and Artificial Intelligence
workers. World-wide technology
was heralded as the great
equalizer for distance, diversity,
and disadvantage.

My husband's prognosis
was progressive decline, like a ship
sinking without a lifeboat. Stiff
muscles fought like brave soldiers
before falling back from the front.
Already surrendered, his left side
slumped. Radio static has replaced
his smooth singing voice. But,

his tremor halted when brain waves
were wired to his chest computer,
a treasure box buried under his
skin that tempts us with a huge fortune,
a return to normalcy, to our pre-disease
life, so like the pleasure of re-reading a favorite book.

How does the Cloud answer
the cries from the Afghan wedding
shootout this past week, leaving 21 dead,
8 wounded? Who does the great equalizer stand with,
the Taliban or the Afghans, in the bloodiest
killing season since 2001?

Truth is fetched, returned, systematized
based on our commands. Tech apps
save us time and effort, but bloodshed
always begs questions, like a beaten dog
begging its master for a reassuring treat.
Can the Cloud save us from
the terrible static of our fists?

Crossroad

The child's chatter arrives before
her fuzzy figure on a bike fills each
video frame on my cell, a second-

hand story of my granddaughter.
She moves from crib toys to bicycle
on unpaved road as I blink at my

phone, the only lifeline that synchs
our distant lives. In my day, I
snailed letters and photos to family

and waited for replies to then old
news, like classmates trying to study
current events. Her mom and I text

more than talk, similar to my old
letters but in real time. We all do
some face time, but it's hard to gather

when we're spread out, unlike
families who used to cluster in one
locale forever. I navigate to stay

close to my clan in this new world,
but face-to-face is still the best
way for me to keep in touch.

What's-her-name

My answering machine is a deaf-mute
that insists on showing no messages

to assure me I'm quite alone when
I open my home door at day's end.

My sadistic mailbox takes pleasure
in crowding current resident posts

through my peephole, like a bait-
and-switch prank, so I think, just for

a moment, that actual people know
my name. I'm convinced junk mailings

try to seduce me with fake importance,
like sweepstake campaigns that want

me to think I'm a winner. My bulk mail
is the greatest pretender, using my real

name, sometimes sincerely handwritten
by a computer, to get me to open it

before it laughs in my face. Until I
became single, I'd never felt bullied,

the butt of cruel jokes, as if an outcast
from the pack. Removing that duo

layer, I feel anonymous, even when
someone or some list knows my name.

Dead Head

A slight slit was the start for
this pageant princess of two
whose mom bought a smile wider
to win her first beauty revue.

Bleaching her teeth was next for
this preschool entrant's bright smile
so she'd have the votes of the judges
and a big win with ivory style.

Then she insisted on smaller ears
this contestant when a driven tween
so snip, tuck and away they went.
She'd do anything to be queen.

Big boobs were the next she bought
this champion in her teens.
For weeks she worked after school
to own the largest ever seen.

Her tummy needed trimming
this college contender espied.
Sucks and tucks gladly done
to grab the victor's landslide.

Make-up tattoos next a must
this twenty-something was sure.
Brows, lashes, lips, eye liner
for the inky allure she'd ensure.

Lifts and injections, fountains of youth
this middle-ager claimed.
New lips, eyes, thighs and butt
concealed her aging frame.

Scalp flaps and hair extensions
this old bag of bones then craved.
Bonded tar-black long tendrils
hid thinning hair she'd repaved.

The time came to pay the price for
this patchwork countess of change.
Countless years playing at pretty
cost her plenty in exchange.

Droopy tattoos slid all askew.
Lifts went south to her feet.
Implants wandered here and there.
Injections flowed to her seat.

Bald-patch weeds grew everywhere.
Gum lifts forced her teeth to escape.
Unfit to eat she fast grew weak
in the skin of a lunar landscape.

Until a plan flashed before her eyes
one last snip would save her.
She'd freeze her head for a century more
and buy beauty in the life hereafter.

Time After Time

A looker in her day,
guys tumbled in her wake.
Her chassis revved notice
drove men wild with a shake.

Beauty used to winning
life – cake and eat it too.
Young bones made it easy
for all dreams to come true.

Time zipped coldly by her,
years amassed overnight.
Failing eyes fooled the mirror,
flawless beauty, so skin tight.

Ruby lips and apple cheek,
all that's left of the flame.
She lives in old movies,
aglow in stale acclaim.

False Face

Many a true word is spoken in jest
                    Shakespeare

mortal words cannot recount
what methinks of you

> *you hoary-headed brute*
> *odorous canker blossom*

to utter sweet nothings
upon leathern wings

> *I'd rather fly into fire*
> *so afeared to look at your oxlips*

abundant beauty beyond
counterfeit good looks

> *you bring deepest loathing to stomach*
> *and your neigh bark grunt slay sleep*

my angel wakes me
bedabbled with the dew

> *crook-kneed and dewlapped wretch*
> *a patched fool in feather trappings*

what visions of you carry me
morn to saucy midsummer's night

> *beneath a fruitless moon*
> *I steal away from this dreadful dole*

Strip Mall Apocalypse

Hunger for profit chops forests, already
fragile from global warming. 137
species die daily, but profiteers deny

devastation as mere seasonal shows,
where the dead return in the second act.
But, the final performance will be

cancelled because disturbed communities
are forever changed. The white-washed
face of urban planning installs three trees

per 10,000 feet, like poster children on
sanitized, verdant stages. We'll be left
with playbills, souvenirs of once live shows –
   wax museums
   movie clips
   stuffed cages.

   Subtle songs
   vibrant colors
   singular scents

will be lost in

   metal
   brick
   glass.

Food Fights

*We're the country that has more food to eat
than any other country in the world, and
with more diets to keep us from eating it.*

Author Unknown

Modern repast rejects provisions
of the past like trash by food
expiration date. Vegetarians multiply
and diversify – from Hallelujah

dieters praising plants from the Holy
Book to Lacto-Ovo herbivores loving
milk and eggs as a lifestyle, not
a one-time event. Fad dieters favor

the latest and greatest, following twitter
bites of the day; medical mealers fork
over the biggest bills, digesting doctored
foods. Fashion-foodies choose paparazzi

cuisine – gluten-free, lactose-free, fat-free,
BPA-free, low-salt, organic, with few
helpings of tasty traditions on the side.
Nobody seems more obsessed by diet

than America, the heavy-weight champ.
If who they are is what they eat, then
vegetarians must not eat anything with
a face. Hallelujah dieters must not defile

their temple with a Budweiser. Lacto-Ovo
herbivores must lead cows and bird
embryos into green pastures. Fad dieters
must welcome trend-setters to the table

with no bellies barred. Medical mealers
must follow nutrition for conditions,
like a boot-camp soldier to pass the muster.
Fashion-foodies must proselytize the latest

trend, like celebrity groupies. Truth
weighs with results, somewhere between
quality and quantity, a tip of the scale,
a second look by the admiring eye.

Ew!

Humans, big germy gumbos
ninety percent blobs of bugs
vs. fleshy cells, the forgotten minority.

Gross habits generate
healthy microbes,
sick stuff stimulating strength!

Yes,

Kiss your dog's mouth!
Bite your nails!
Suck your baby's pacifier!
Take fewer showers!

What?

Pet parasites   nail bits   gunky binkies   watery robbers of skin oils
are all commandos against infirmed invaders!

But,

Don't play with zits or scabs!
Don't eat boogers!
Don't hawk phlegm in public!
Don't sneeze-spray the world!

Why?

Pus   nose glop   spittle   gushers   ulcerated secretions
None are your bosom buddies!

So,
Choose your friends wisely. Know
your real enemies. Don't
let your body surrender!

Class Act

A is
line leader
best grade
teacher's pet
dictionary demagogue
ruling class

B, C, D, E are
students after "A"
second bests
always bridesmaids
passable efforts
plain Janes

F is
student failure
social outcast
pitiable pawn
sullen footman
impoverished fool

G, H, J, Q are
disenfranchised expats
handicapped relatives
innocent scapegoats
naive fugitives
cautious introverts

I, K, L, N, T, V, W are
straight-line militants
TV evangelists
rule-makers
black-and-whites
stoic bureaucrats

M is
lost middle child
peace mediator
average Joe
moderate politician
fence straddler

P, R are
sharp marketers
glad handers
baby kissers
reckless gamblers
charismatic politicos

O, S, U are
slippery deceivers
fickle chameleons
incorrigible deviants
convincing actors
strident Machiavellis

X, Y are
sex symbols
undercover aliens
mythical creatures
random factors
math genomes

Z is
bottom of the heap
hapless after-thought
hopeless dead-end
foot soldier
obedient supporter

Political Whiskers – Tiny, Frayed Threads from Raw Seam Edges

We look at life from the back side of the tapestry.
and most of the time, what we see are
loose threads, tangled knots and the like.
-John Piper

Double Take

The Towers
tumbled thousands,
only bloodless ash
left for tombstones.

Feelings frozen
stiff sinews
of relentless demise.

No negotiations just
loving the living
grieving the gone.

The Comfort of Elsewhere

*Egypt bombed Libya, hours after the militants'
beheadings of 21 Egyptian Christians.*

I'm no war criminal. Why do these bloody
headlines scream at me while I'm trying to pay
for my damn Starbucks? Let those ragheads kill
each other for all I care. They've been doin' it
for centuries... hah, like I can make a difference.
What BS! How much? What's up with tax
on coffee? Here, I've got the penny.

I am too familiar with this rollercoaster ride,
the liberal media always imagining the end
of the world. I gotta remind myself newspapers
are in the business of making money. Shit sells.
Monstrous firework bombs, my ass. I have
to remember it's not real – one more appetizer
to get me to buy more.

Besides, they're so far away, it's not worth my
heartburn since there's absolutely nothing,
nothing, I can do about it!

*Estimated 200 shots in Copenhagen café leave
one dead, three injured. Among survivors,
cartoonist Lars Vilks attending a free speech debate.*

Why do people deliberately put themselves
in hot spots? I am so blessed to be planted
in American soil with so few threats, compared
to the crazy pestilence elsewhere. Blessed
with the right to bear arms to protect myself
unlike those people over in Norway, or was it

Finland, who didn't shoot back. I thank God
on my US of A knees for blessing
my Midwestern stronghold!

*Despite the February ceasefire, gunfire along
the frontline does not seem to have ceased at all.
The Ukrainian army continues to lose soldiers
on a daily basis.*

I admit my best friend in high school was
Ukrainian, but I need a ceasefire myself from
all this news just to avoid the downer drama
of those people. Oh, I feel bad, really bad,
for the Ukrainians, for anybody who has to put up
with Russians as next-door neighbors. Jesus,
I'm glad I built in a different neighborhood.
I want my martini, stirred, not shaken up by
Bolshevik bullshit!

*American troops…told to share quarters
with extremist Iran-backed Shiite militias in Iraq,
the people murdering them with roadside bombs
just a few years ago.*

I'm turning my friggin' car radio off. Who
needs this crap in morning traffic! We spent all
this money on these people to free them and this
is the thanks we get for being a good role model
of democracy during our ten-year occupation.
I'm no expert to question boots-on-the-ground
judgments by American generals. They always
have our best interests at heart. Oh, man, I'm
gonna be late for work.

Former colonial France back in Mali as police keeper… France Says Troops Killed Qaeda Commander in Mali.

Really? Can you believe it? Radio news at work?
I feel like one of those refugees myself, running
to avoid the trauma bombs hurled at the world.
I wish somebody would invent a dis-entanglement
device like an answering machine screening
calls from those millions elsewhere interrupting
my part of the world.

Keffiyeh

1,000 children in the West Bank
arrested every year for crimes
against Israel, the face of innocence

no longer safe. Among the annual
200 imprisoned Palestinian kids,
Khatib is the youngest of only four

girls behind bars, a curious jail cell
culprit. After 45 days in prison, her
smile charms the camera as she

poses for the press, perhaps a seductive
lion cub hiding killer instincts. Her
black-and-white checkered scarf,

popular among young Arab patriots,
is like an innocent band t-shirt, or
perhaps like telltale underground

resistance. Is Khatib a sinless
concert-goer caught in the cross-hairs
of armed conflict or a new recruit

against war as a way of life? Perhaps
the more useful question is
why are we even asking our children?

World Hunger
hip-hop

greed loaded
reloaded
innocent or not
shot
shots spraying
wounded baying

no time to recoil
oil's the spoil
winners get richer
neighbors in danger
nowhere to hide
desires decide

the not guilty
guilty
being in the way
their heads flayed
parents lost
kids bear cost

variation
an aberration
be the same or die
run, hide or lie
refugees bloodied
too many buried

allies always switch
based on who's rich
Arabs fight each other
Jews now their brothers
Europe loves and hates
the States, watches and waits

century to century
wealth-seeking countries
recruit young fighters
waving patriot banners
people used for gains
sovereign wealth reigns

Blood Money
hip-hop

Latin isles, Injun lands
Arab oil, Asian trade
Many die, greed expands
Kill for cash, freedom flayed

People rise playin' god
Hitler's Reich, Mau Tse's Reds
Ho Chi Minh, now Assad
Pick a side, we're all dead

Here we are once again
Actin' like world police
Takin heat to defend
Makin' war never peace

Ninety-two battles fought
Major wars, eighteen count
Ev'ry three, we take shots
Millions dead, world account

Chemi-bombs killed their own
News reports, rumors grow
Syrian dead and world moans
US points, Assad's foe

Here we are once again
Actin' like world police
Takin heat to defend
Makin' war never peace

The world waits, we decide
Same old place, do or die
England's out, Allies bide
US in (or) big bad guy

Syrian oil, truth be told
Not their dead, merely pawns
Makes the world, stand so bold
Get US (to) bomb at dawn

Here we are once again
Actin' like world police
Takin' heat to defend
Makin' war never peace

High-Rent Neighborhood

Centuries are joined at the gut
by appetite, no shelter from the reach
of grandstand gluttony. Every arcade
touts the Pollyanna shell game
for chump change that falls easily
from pocket holes. Regimented, dark

clouds amass strikes well-hidden
by bannered, patriotic high-five slaps.
Recruits in cheap rooms with no view
maneuver land minds, their innocence
charred by nationalistic wildfires.
Wealth leaps to undisturbed pastures

of milk and honey smoothies,
insinuates molotovs among bystanders
for dollar crops. Thin-wrapped faith
is prone to torn jumbled paper money
but solidifies in the daze of deliberate
ritual to hide real costs.

The homeland is kept safe by uniformed
thinkers who use stage make-up
and archeological props to maintain
mass enchantment. Myth is prolonged
by the poor's delusion that wealth
is possible for anyone who works.

No Sense Nonsense
hip-hop

Try as I might, do as I should
Look past the facts, would if I could.
Nothing matters, I'm one in a crowd.
It's not my doing, no fault allowed.

War after war, load and reload,
Faceless bodies, hatred explodes.
Centuries bleed, one to another.
Righteous cause hides greed, the crusher.

Ancient Rome and Greece, lived by wars –
Blood baths in Europe and African shores.
Brits, Italians, Spanish, Portuguese –
Treasures from natives, taken with ease.

Modern combat, more of the same,
Noble and just, only in name.
Nuclear bombs and chemical warfare,
Stakes are higher, death everywhere.

Jihad radicals, Syrian rebels,
Korean plutonium, Chinese generals.
Ain't it awful say pointed fingers.
Good and bad guys, fake justice lingers.

Nam war protests, my youth's soup de jour –
Believing right from wrong, we were cocksure.
No longer savvy, can't see what to do.
Death lives on, awaits me and you.

Pigmentocracy

I recognize Jesus in a custom Armani
driving his Mercedes-Benz CL65
in heavenly Beverly Hills. He is White.
Believers emulate by bleaching their skin.

Devotees beget a universal frenzy of faith –
whitening flesh, rounding eyes, narrowing noses.
The global god is White too. South African coloureds,
lighter Latins, Eurocentric Arabs, pale Asians.

Our nation is under god, the same White guy.
Less black-looking blacks, or any colors
closer to the guy's,
reap divine sanction from the flock.

My Filipino father followed Jesus to freedom land –
bleached his hands, married whites, westernized his
clothes, tongued English, baptized a naturalized
citizen – went to heaven of the American Dream.

Flip Side
hip-hop

Neighborhood makes
or breaks.
Philippinos have high
real estate stakes
a popular place
with world politicos,
just the tip of Flip
island woes.

Indians
(Asian not
American-soiled)
conquered
religionized
sperm-a-cized
to and fro,

followed by Brits
then Conquistadores

different faces
but same hungry
whores.

Three centuries
of Spanish catechism
fell to blue-eyed Americanism
til 1902
when US
pledged Flips
first freedoms too
in '45

but World War
delayed the cries
liberty not til '46.

Yet fine print let
US bases stay,
that's what's called
the American way

til '92
when activists
succeeded,
booted Uncle Sam
although that's debated.

Still some military
presence as advisors,
using exercisers –
that is, military games
it's a matter of names.

Let's not forget drones
since 2002
war on terror
takes no sympathizer.

Then there's UAVs
weaponized
to tease
Asian or Islam
on the Seas,
especially
the South China Sea.

Overt or CIA covert
drones in Pakistan, Somalia
and Philippines,
a checkerboard game,
safety by any means.

Now Obama in 2014
with President Aquino
making it seem
public cooperation
between the two nations
wanting peace among all Asians

through return of US troops
to secure any gaps and loops,
regional peace and security-
I feel safer, are you with me?

Tempest

Gut-wrenching stench of grief
resides in rags on survivors. Stunned
eyes search debris for faint breath
under miles of Haiyan's rubble.

Death toll more than 4,000,
another 13 million half-dead –
homeless, orphaned, injured,
starved, mentally erased.

At the archipelago's center,
Leyte endured worst punches –
its major cities on their knees,
half its people gone missing.

Homeless scrounge survival
with makeshift meals from scraps,
day-long waits for pimply promises –
meds, shelter, news of the dead.

Fear of further disease causes
burials before identification,
survivors haunted by questions –
never knowing, forever mourning.

March 11, 2011
hip-hop

Three years more and no one's found three melted cores
Fukushima's radiation still soars, dangerously pours
death breaks down Japan, knocking door to door
and now laps upon our once safely far US shores.

300 tons of waste still flowing today,
scores of tons more in containers each day.
Pay-offs to crime bosses add clean-up delays
as downwind victims have no say in finding their way.

The worst is the deadly kids storm born.
Thyroid cancer forms 40 times the norm.
Nodules and cysts advance too fast to forewarn,
so 46 percent of youth die, innocence deformed.

Those reactors and 30 more are now closed
for not meeting new standards Japan imposed,
but you should know 60 plus in US exposed
for running far below Japan's belated codes.

Plants on faults in LA, San Fran and NYC
are seismic threats for both ends of our country.
Last June, nuke waste blew a New Mexico facility
and all poor locals were contaminated quickly.

So why no news of Japan's continued bald tragedy?
Does global nuke money hold the answer key?
Does Japan's plight pose a threat to big money?
What will it take to make welfare of all priority?

Old Miss Libertas

*Give me your tired, your poor/Your huddled masses
yearning to breathe free/The wretched refuse of your
teeming shore/Send these, the homeless, tempest-tost
to me/I lift my lamp beside the golden door.*
                                                  Emma Lazarus

Bones lecture more boldly with age, muscles
slouching in surrender when she stands too long,
her dutiful right arm rising stiffly to greet visitors.

Still sharp, she recalls her immigration, surrounded
by only French gentlemen (ladies then excluded)
welcoming her to a new job, a new homeland.

She stood for freedom of huddled masses,
but knew instinctvely she'd champion women's
inalienable rights – life, liberty, happiness.

Celebrating women when they won the right
to vote, again when they gained legal equality in jobs,
school and health, her joy fast deflated in tidal lawsuits.

The Supreme Court now allows corporations
to restrict women's rights – hold healthcare hostage,
lock up lifestyles, choke childcare.

Women are second-class citizens without voice
in paychecks, top jobs, even abuse in their own homes.
Equality is as elusive as the day Miss Libertas arrived.

Writing on the Wall

Trace chalk dust memorializes
my childhood blackboard. Washable,

no-muss markers replace broken
crayons in tin cans in my old

Chicago brick school house.
Capital and lower-case cursive

letters on my elementary class
walls pushed penmanship, no

longer required by tech teaching
and digitized communication.

I input my password on today's
screen to catch news bytes, poke

family and friends, travel to virtual
Ireland, and print anything – guns to

gowns, from my 3D printer. The only
scene that hasn't changed since

I was a Windy City school girl is
the news – Russian-American tension,

Arab-Israeli conflict, world hunger,
end-of-the-world pollution. Will there

be an app developed to fix
the human condition?

Corrupted Innocence

In the deadening stillness of cease-fire, Abdul
looks for his toys in the rubble. Basira digs

for simple trinkets coveted in a box under her
bed in nameless bits and pieces called home.

Yasmin, 6, in Gaza City, has endured three wars
in her lifetime. She wonders, without emotion,

where she will lay tonight. Awake or asleep, she
lives the fear of wolfish wounds, nowhere safe.

These children are lucky to be the living dead,
always lived in war like cooped chickens,

ignorant of fresh air. Four cousins playing near
the harbor, two brothers in a taxi with grandma,

one four-year-old and his eight-year-old brother
inside their house, a three-year-old playing with dad

in the family garden, and a boy and father going
to mosque – all dead before this brief pause

in the war as if snuffed between cigarettes. Young
global nomads bicycle bombed-out streets, kick

rag balls outside makeshift medical tents, feed
beat-up dolls with pretend food to play out their fate.

Math for Girls Counts

Before they were great, great grandmothers, they stood in prolonged
lines for singular equality, where one scale weighed the importance
of each person by numbers, blind to gender, creed or color. But,

the Land of the Free delayed women voting until 1920, 144 years
after propertied White men, 51 years after Black men, as if women
were merely household amenities. The Nineteenth Amendment did

move the whole line one step closer to pointing out discrepancies in
economic and reproductive solutions, but their corrections were
often erased as emotional hyperbole by irrational females, the errors

with them, not with the system. In 1936, birth control info, no longer
labeled obscene, could be mailed in plain brown envelopes but
addressed to husbands, as if a married man were the only Good

Housekeeping Seal of Approval. Connecticut's 1965 defeat allowed
the pill but, again, for wedded couples. I knew unmarried, pregnant girls
who were shamed, blamed for bad choices with boys who were just being

boys, used to getting their way, for two hundred years. The 1982 states'
defeat of the ERA countered the gains made by women voting, just sixty
years earlier. Today, the same fifteen states have still not ratified, almost

one hundred years since women's suffrage. The ERA loss meant I had
no credit, no bank account, no property without my husband's name,
addressed as Mrs. John Doe, without mention of even my first name as

a person. Despite 1973's Roe vs. Wade for abortion, women's reproductive
rights have been removed from the equation by corporations now controlling
choice as newly-deemed religious bodies, more like a catch-22 where women

have zero say. Yet, women keep getting back up when delayed, detoured, even derailed by the centuries-old male monopoly. They've done the math, know equal means equal, not less than, and insist on the right answer.

Global Darning – Repairing Holes or Worn Areas

*It is threads, hundreds of tiny threads,
which sew people together through the years.*
                                    Simon Signoret

Lunch Encounter

Across from me, a Kurdish refugee, now in D.C., eats pizza. The Cairo woman says she detects his slight American speech while she tries pancakes with a hot dog. Left of me, a Jamaican eats a vegetarian plate as he pitches his show, Food War, at small colleges before his visa expires. Two New Yorkers, one Brooklyn and one Bronx, are picking at food, intent on conversation with the Egyptian who's showing cell phone pictures of her brother and his fiancé who is too good for him. Another vegetarian, a Filipino woman from California, and her new Virginia friend join our table, sitting next to an African-American physician-writer from Philadelphia, who piles salt on his buffet choices. Between bites, the three anecdote segregation where each lives. I am raving about how wonderful the sautéed garlic spinach is, occasionally interjecting my personal experiences as a bi-racial child in the trio's diatribe. Drifting in and out of each other's ordinary conversations, we shrink the globe to plate size.

Mixed Woodland

My cousin is more my brother
like long-lost twins never really
apart. Our histories are written
in volumes on the same shelf.

My oldest friend is a trusted
sister, our blood transfused
from shared defeats and triumphs
since our teens.

My Aunt Etta is my mom, also Barbara,
my Sunday School teacher, and therapist,
Glory B. (her real name), to choose
a few of the women who've fed me.

Countless school children, colleagues
and neighbors are my babies, my cousins,
my aunts and uncles. They are my family,
a hearty tree I planted myself.

One tree was not enough to provide
stability, shelter, and sustenance. I
went to the forest for what I needed,
from many different trees.

Universal Language

Two million years of musical
rhythm compose visceral
understanding underneath

man's survival stance,
a spontaneous response like turtle
hatchlings drawn to sea.

Even before language, melodic
tempos captured all cultures,
a human flesh denominator.

In the womb, the unborn dance
to notes and beats – inherent
as honey bees dancing towards

a food source. Harmonics tie
all groups. People move
in collective excitement, all cued

by rhythms, internalized as one
jukebox. Concerts, marches, dirges
choreograph brain waves

like birds in formation,
like fish in schools,
like monarchs in migration.

Tune transcends disease. People
with aphasia sing, with Tourette's
drum, with retardation dance,

with dementia remember. Music
fights back. Man's humanity survives
without symbol or instruction.

Cold War Corner

Neighborhoods of immigrants
wrestled with American rebirth.

Italians in guineas muscled
to the front of the food line.

The Irish joined police ranks
to vent bloodlust for the Brits.

Poles lived behind store fronts,
peddled blood soup and pierogis.

Jews sold resettled dignity
in familiar old world trinkets.

Newcomers sputtered English,
children often their translators.

Settlement houses mothered the new,
interpreted the fast-talking landscape.

Schools promised shiny gold stars,
better lives than parents suffered.

Desperate jobs were prized, seen
as a foot in the door of hope.

The American Dream remains
the touchstone for seekers without home.

Living Large

Manhattan skyline
erect as cold nipples
perked to attention by
the gray December bite.

New Yorkers rush past
stop lights, honking cabbies.
Stony faces
snake to boroughs.

Hustlers fish
for tourist trout,
an easy-catch meal.

Two-bit waiters daydream
of tickets to redemption,
a Broadway spotlight.

Wall Street feeds on
desperate dollars
of last-chance gamblers.

Hungry immigrants grab
chances for their young
from rubble to worth.

Fat, burly New York City
panders the American Dream
on every street corner.

The Apple promises all –
anonymity has no history,
anyone becomes anybody,
Ambition need only apply.

Unseen Seen

*It is not freedom from conditions, but it is freedom
to take a stand toward the conditions.*
                                         Viktor E. Frankl

Senses sift thoughts into maps, create ways to sojourn Mother
Earth. Bundled perceptions lend contrived sensibility to choices

amidst fickle realities, like the timeless myth of the 24-hour day.
We force delinquent minutes to hide behind time zones so clocks

seem in step with the sun since earth's real elliptical orbit throws
out regularity. Evolution is another man-made hyperbole. Superiority

and complexity are mere card tricks. Winning fungi, sharks, mosses
have had the same hand for a millennia. Science popularizes

discoveries in fifteen-minute frames of fame. Aristotle made celebrities
of vision, sound, smell, touch and taste when he brought them

to the stage, but there are fifteen sensory performers including
temperature, time, thirst, pain and pressure, who should be given

credit. Truth is not absolute, more a shape shifter of coerced image.
Sky wears blue disguising multi-colored diversity. Weather-beaten

brains do not surrender learning as old headlines declared. Today's
truth is more dead reckoning of position from distance run.

Do we forge direction without all confirmed colors of life's prism
to free ourselves from the prison of changing circumstance?

Newlyweds 96 & 95
True Story

asleep, my whole
body   smiles   broadly
  unconscious
but aware he rests near
an   unspoken comfort
with a partner
  who shares
my extant fingerprint

companionship   cushions
old bones   confronting   time
  my foggy vision
guided by his   headlight sight
  his fumbling feet
supported by my   steady pace
  his dulled hearing
enlightened by   my good ear

yet ageless   hearts thrive
in common ground
we dance   to music
  most   don't remember
walk on   familiar clay
  from kindred childhoods
laugh   in one breath
  without words exchanged

our love   cannot   be stolen
by mere facts
  fallible limbs   unfaithful memory
nor by blunt events
  Black-White bias   hungry heirs
our hearts   cannot   be emptied

Global Spectrum

Different skin tones   scatter us,
dandelion seeds   toss
in the wind.
Primary colors live
in less segregation,
isolation is softened to   muted truce.

Boxed absolutes
raise questions,
jumbled tints
challenge   old truths.
The cronies of   barbed
rules retire,
new jobs arise to   mixed multitudes.

Increasing range of flesh tones
breaks ground,
levels field for   all shades of children.
The color-blind eye of
diversity
frames a portrait of
one world family.

Penny the Shrimp
(after Penaeus Setiferus, White Shrimp)

White shrimp spawning in Gulf water swells
A million purple eggs straight to bottom fell.
Itsy bitsy larvae all hatched in half a day.
One rare shrimp arose to show them the way.

Her name was Penny but mighty for her size.
As a baby, she survived many dangers in disguise.
Immortal styrofoam and plastics in the sea,
big fish and loggerheads wouldn't let her be.

She learned tough lessons, man was not a friend.
Farmers and builders, tourists all pretend.
Mother Earth's bounty would always be at hand,
nothing need be done, no actions ever banned.

Penny drew the young, from fish to octopi,
called land critters and all birds that fly,
led them to deep water or some remote place.
Their absence brought panic, folks talked face to face.

They all worked together to respect Mother Earth.
Penny showed the loss, if Earth was not first.
Sky is the limit when you stand up for what's true.
Big and small matters, keeping Earth green and blue.

United We Stand

over colored fences
through locked religions
past anti-age bombs
beyond rules etched on tombstones
we bleed the same blood

No Dead Roots

Silk plants are problem-free companions like Internet
friends. These ageless beauties have no demands.
They do not talk back, wait patiently to add, never
take, like a geisha paid to please. You are the center
of their universe. There is no worry when you go away,

no pet-sitting fees to pay. They are always there
to welcome you back. It is much easier to imitate life
with fake plants than to live in the dirty mess of keeping
real plants alive. Phony plants take up no valuable time.
Neutered garland needs no water nor food. Silky imposters

can be enjoyed without the least affection expected
in return like plastic dolls on a display shelf. Silks stay
young on the stem forever. Buds maintain blush
in perennial springtime like actors in a vintage movie.
Ripe petals enjoy mature wisdom with no suspicion

of sagging decline. Leaves sustain verdant vitality
without the inconvenient burnt edges of real life. Rootless,
there is no emotional mud when you tire of them, only
the trash heap. Yet, the faintest scent of fresh plant life
enriches all living things. Food and water added

to authentic greenery brings vibrant response, hopeful
shoots to savor, much like watching a grandchild grow.
Life's changing colors help us cope with mortality
like mile markers along the path. Time spent nurturing
real roots sweetens our sense of belonging to everything.

Openhanded
True Story

Breath weeps from the dumpster
umbilical mother cut free from burden –
unwashed guilt, judgment, shamed regret.

Soft tears voiced from mucous opening
muted by human leavings stuck to his skin –
trash tossed unwelcomed, unvalued.

Acceptance born before innocence –
surrendered to abide or slip away
while patient vermin stir nearby.

But, something disturbs rubble's stench.
An officer's hand cradles release,
rescues a fragile four-pound lifetime.

Newborn, now man, meets the man,
twenty-five years since his re-birth that day,
from rubble to salvaged treasure.

Way of Looking

There are always flowers for those who want to see them.
                                        Henri Matisse

Sadie surprised everyone when she came
to the holiday party because hospice care
deflated expectations like a child not

chosen for the team. Wearing her best-
dressed smile, she mingled and sampled
fancy finger foods, the most Miss Manners

she could muster. Her last public
appearance, she gave a generous goodbye.
Vera's place sat empty for months

before her children felt up to selling,
the final ritual of farewell. She had returned
from an Alaskan adventure before cancer

prevailed like a dogged nor'easter.
No one has met the new old lady. Winter
holds hostages, hunkered behind

locked doors of rations, but she drives
a red-hot convertible and wears wild
boots, according to grizzled busybodies.

Married sixty-some years, Don and Ella,
hiked and biked the Rockies with kids,
then grandkids, along amiable streams

of good health. They settled here painting
watercolors of world travels, sold as cards
in local shops. The week before palliative

care, Don rolled his wheel-chair chariot
around the block to chit-chat and joke
since old-habits refuse to die.

When Renaissance Rosie couldn't sculpt, she
took up ceramics, then painting. For her
ninetieth, she drank champagne side-saddle

on back of a Harley, like any other biker girl,
hot to ride. Starting poetry in her mid-
nineties, she published two collections

before ninety-eight. She was making
friends with the surgical nurse when she
finally stopped. Befriended

by this multi-faceted gem, assorted
hundreds attended her send-off party
that would have delighted Da Vinci.

Before moving, they'd rented an apartment
with a balcony view of the dumpster,
transformed into Shangri-La by her fifty

tropical plants. Here, Peggy adopted
mountain wildflowers to soften the loss
of Florida-kissed perennials. Gus turned

to an electric instead of his faithful
acoustic when his hands refused
to cooperate like willful two-year-olds

running amok. With artsy hearts,
they both write despite the weather
forecast of progressive disease.

No Pain, All Gain?

No-work wishes are fulfilled
with fast fixes and snips for
bug eyes
big bottoms
tiny tits.

Science and business fight obesity
profiting from the push for easy skinny
tummy tubes
intestinal barriers
dual-signal drugs.

Lab formulas make it easy
to eat on automatic pilot
cheek swabs
genetic profiles
sci-fad diets.

Losses dive deep under shallow skin
with damages resurfacing later
hearts
guts
brains.

But, some individuals choose
different beauty marks
senior triathlonists
octogenarian yogis
autistic authors.

Choice defines us, actions
carve character. Easy is
not always what it seems.

One Line to Live

Life is not a straight line,
Nor a tidy row of dashes.
It's more a series of periods
With question marks and slashes.

Sometimes the commas give
Us pause to glimpse our substance
As we ponder obscure asterisks
In search of God's existence.

There must be more to life
Than tight colons and their lists
Some secrets in parentheses
Revealing way to bliss.

It's easy to live by
Another's quotation marks,
Hide in dark backspaces
Than write personal remarks.

I choose to live my life,
One line per situation,
Risk grammar and spelling errors,
Trust my own punctuation.

ACKNOWLEDGEMENTS

Select poems in some form have appeared in other publications:

Cutthroat, Online Journal, 2015: "empty fridge"
Their Own Bare Hands, Unbound Content, 2015: "One Line to Live," "Jalopy," "A Sort of Self"
Healing Muse, SUNY Press, 2014: "emptying"
Today & Yesterday, Online Journal, Laughing Fire Press, 2014: "Wallet," "Club Membership"
The Truth About the Fact, Loyola Marymount Press, 2013: "Twitnomenon," "Global Spectrum"
Reckless Writing, Chatter House Press, 2013: "Fallen Leaves"
Second Monday Muse, South Florida Group Ten, 2013: "One Line to Live"
Female First, UK's Female First Online Journal 2012: "Dead Head"
Lip Service, Miami Actors' Playhouse, 2012: "Believe"

Select poems in some form have won awards at state or national level:

Poetry Society of Virginia, 2014: "Penny the Shrimp"
National Federation of State Poetry Societies, 2013: "One Line to Live," "A Sort of Self"
Florida State Poetry Association, 2013: "Back Talk"
Virginia Writers Club, 2013: "Tramp"
Florida State Poetry Association, 2012: "Tramp"

Select poems in some form have been featured at guest readings at the state, national, or international level:

Actors Playhouse, Coral Gables, Florida
Bridgewater International Poetry Festival
Dead or Alive Poets

Florida State Poetry Association
International Mother Language Day Poetry Celebration
Live Poets
Miami Soiree
100,000 Poets for Change
Piedmont Community College
Poetry Society of Virginia
Rapunzel's
South Florida Writers Association
SWAG Writers
Virginia Writers Club

I thank my friends, mentors, and especially my husband, George Phillips, for their generous support, encouragement, and inspiration.

ABOUT THE AUTHOR

The first in her family to finish high school, Patsy Asuncion had a successful public school career, from teacher to principal. Upon retirement, grants and program development skills morphed into pleasure writing – poetry and short stories. After decades in south Florida, she lives in Virginia where she is active in her community promoting diversity through the arts – hosting an open mic for artists of all ages and skin tones, as well as helping to organize local writer events for peace initiatives. As a caregiver herself, Patsy also hosts a Parkinson's support group. She loves being closer to her children and grandchildren from Virginia to Massachusetts!

CPSIA information can be obtained
at www.ICGtesting.com
Printed in the USA
FSOW02n0223060516
20119FS

9 780996 490528